Dedicated to all individuals receiving care from Duffy Health Center: past, present, future.

Table of Contents

I have the privilege of knowing Melissa Payne and Jeremy Wurzburg through their critically important work as Recovery Support Navigators at Duffy Health Center. Both Melissa and Jeremy identify as individuals in sustained recovery, and they bring the power of their own lived experiences to their roles.

Through their interactions with the patients they serve, I have witnessed their compassionate approach as well as their incredible creativity. This creativity - paired with the drive to reduce stigma towards individuals experiencing homelessness, struggling with their mental health, and at times battling substance use disorders - served as the catalyst for the creation of *Perfectly Different Faces*.

Melissa's love of writing and her experience in early childhood education provided the poetic stage; Jeremy's personal love for art and his work as a peer mentor within an adolescent expressive arts program resulted in the beautiful illustrations within this story.

Thank you, Melissa and Jeremy, for empowering our patients through some of the most challenging periods in their lives, while also celebrating the successes in their process. And thank you for the gift of *Perfectly Different Faces*.

Daniel Rodrigues, LICSW
Associate Director of Substance Use Disorder Services, Duffy Health Center
August 2020

Perfectly Different Faces

The Earth is home to such beautiful sites:

Oceans, mountains, and big city lights.

The most magical part of all these places

Are the many perfectly different faces.

Each person has something that makes them unique.

A silly laugh, sparkling eyes, or big rosy cheeks.

There's a different story behind each name.

So many journeys, not one is the same.

Some people have houses and lots of stuff.

And others have not nearly enough.

There are people who live in a car or the woods

With no place to snuggle or hang their hoods.

See, everyone deserves a place to call home,

To learn, grow, and keep their comb.

Homelessness is not okay, and that's a fact.

We can't look away, it's time to act.

In little Massachusetts,

there's a place called Cape Cod.

That's where you'll find

the Duffy Health Center squad.

Duffy provides care to those in need.

They work to supply the tools to succeed.

Kindness, compassion, big smiles, and more;

Open minds, brain power, teamwork galore!

There are a few important things

Duffy knows to be true,

Beliefs that make them awesome in all that they do.

Each special someone should have food and clothes,

Along with health care and

shelter when it rains or snows.

When things are hard, there is so much to do.

So Duffy is there to walk through it, too.

They know it's not easy to ask

For someone to help you complete a tough task.

They work together with their neighbors in town

To find ways to help people be safe and sound.

What makes Duffy great is their passion for people

And the wonderful way they treat everyone equal.

You see, just because a person has nowhere to live

Does not mean they've done something

you wouldn't forgive.

So let's say hooray for the Duffy team's plan

To always be willing to help when we can!

The mission of Duffy Health Center is to provide comprehensive, integrated health care and support services to persons who are experiencing homelessness or are at risk of homelessness on Cape Cod, and to improve the quality of life for vulnerable populations through community collaborations, leadership, and advocacy.

At Duffy Health Center, we believe:

1. Homelessness is unacceptable.

2. Every person has the right to food, clothing, housing, and health care.

3. All individuals are capable of change and personal growth.

4. Individuals experiencing homelessness or who are at risk of homelessness have complex needs.

5. Effective treatment means meeting people at their point of need as they define it and supporting their participation in decisions affecting their lives.

6. Safety, health, and stability are the foundation on which other life goals and accomplishments are based.

Melissa Payne, *Author*

Melissa is a Recovery Support Navigator at Duffy Health Center. She holds her Associate degree from Cape Cod Community College, and is working towards her Bachelor's degree in Public Administration at the University of Massachusetts, Amherst.

Melissa has lived experience with substance use disorders and has been in sustained recovery for the past 6 years. This firsthand knowledge allows her to build meaningful relationships with her patients, as they know she was once in their position.

Before joining Duffy Health Center, Melissa was a site director for a school-age program for low income and at-risk children. In her personal time, she writes children's stories that broach sensitive subjects to promote empathy and provide a supportive outlet for children who identify with the subject matter. Melissa is dedicated to advocacy work as well as serving her community. She is passionate about many facets of human services and hopes to continue making an impact as she grows professionally.

Jeremy Wurzburg, *Illustrator*

Jeremy is a Recovery Support Navigator at Duffy Health Center, and a Peer Recovery Mentor at the RecoveryBuild Alternative Peer Group.

He has years of experience in the field of addiction treatment and prevention, working with young adults from all walks of life, and personal experience with his own recovery.

Jeremy has worked as a Recovery Aide at Gosnold, a Youth Mentor at the Creative Outlets program at Cape Cod Museum of Art, and as a Student Mentor at the Provincetown Art Association and Museum.

Jeremy is passionate about art and its use in addictions treatment. He enjoys drawing, hiking, and spending time with his dog.

Made in the USA
Middletown, DE
11 October 2020